EMMANUEL JOSEPH

From Silicon to Soul, A Christian's Guide to Career, Relationships, and AI

Copyright © 2025 by Emmanuel Joseph

All rights reserved. No part of this publication may be reproduced, stored or transmitted in any form or by any means, electronic, mechanical, photocopying, recording, scanning, or otherwise without written permission from the publisher. It is illegal to copy this book, post it to a website, or distribute it by any other means without permission.

First edition

This book was professionally typeset on Reedsy. Find out more at reedsy.com

Contents

1. Chapter 1: The Intersection of Faith and Technology — 1
2. Chapter 2: Navigating the Digital Workplace — 3
3. Chapter 3: Building Strong Relationships in a Digital Age — 5
4. Chapter 4: AI and the Future of Work — 7
5. Chapter 5: Ethical Considerations in AI Development — 9
6. Chapter 6: AI in Ministry and Outreach — 11
7. Chapter 7: Balancing Technology and Spiritual Growth — 13
8. Chapter 8: Raising Children in a Digital World — 15
9. Chapter 9: The Role of AI in Healthcare — 17
10. Chapter 10: AI and Education — 19
11. Chapter 11: The Future of AI and the Church — 21
12. Chapter 12: Embracing the Future with Faith — 23
13. Chapter 13: AI and the Environment — 25
14. Chapter 14: AI and Humanitarian Aid — 27
15. Chapter 15: AI and Mental Health — 29
16. Chapter 16: AI and Ethical Leadership — 31

1

Chapter 1: The Intersection of Faith and Technology

In today's rapidly evolving world, technology has become an integral part of our daily lives. As Christians, we must navigate this digital landscape with a sense of purpose and discernment. Our faith provides us with a unique perspective on how to engage with technology in a way that honors God and enhances our spiritual growth. In this chapter, we will explore the importance of integrating faith and technology, and how we can use digital tools to strengthen our relationship with God and serve others.

At the heart of the Christian faith is the belief that we are created in the image of God, with a unique purpose and calling. This understanding should guide our approach to technology and innovation. By recognizing the potential for both good and harm in technological advancements, we can make informed decisions that align with our values and principles. We will delve into the ethical considerations of technology use, and how to strike a balance between embracing innovation and maintaining our spiritual integrity.

Furthermore, we will examine the role of technology in our personal and professional lives. From social media to artificial intelligence, we must be mindful of how these tools impact our relationships, work, and overall well-being. By approaching technology with a Christ-centered mindset, we can leverage its benefits while avoiding potential pitfalls. This chapter will provide practical tips for using technology in a way that fosters spiritual growth and strengthens our witness to others.

Lastly, we will explore the concept of digital discipleship. In an age where online interactions are becoming increasingly prevalent, we have a unique opportunity to share the love of Christ with a global audience. By leveraging digital platforms, we can reach people who may never set foot in a church, offering them hope and encouragement through our online presence. This chapter will offer strategies for effective digital evangelism and the importance of maintaining authenticity in our online interactions.

2

Chapter 2: Navigating the Digital Workplace

The modern workplace is increasingly dominated by digital tools and remote work. As Christians, we must adapt to these changes while maintaining our commitment to excellence and integrity. In this chapter, we will explore the challenges and opportunities presented by the digital workplace, and how we can thrive in this new environment.

One of the key challenges of the digital workplace is maintaining a healthy work-life balance. With the lines between work and personal life becoming increasingly blurred, it is essential to establish boundaries and prioritize self-care. We will discuss practical strategies for managing time effectively, setting boundaries, and maintaining a sense of balance in our lives. By doing so, we can prevent burnout and ensure that we are able to serve others effectively.

In addition to maintaining balance, we must also consider the ethical implications of our work. As Christians, we are called to act with integrity and uphold ethical standards in all aspects of our professional lives. This chapter will delve into the ethical considerations of working in a digital environment, including issues related to privacy, data security, and responsible use of technology. By adhering to ethical principles, we can build trust and credibility in our workplaces and beyond.

Furthermore, we will explore the importance of fostering meaningful connections in the digital workplace. While technology has made it easier to collaborate and communicate, it can also lead to feelings of isolation and disconnection. This chapter will offer tips for building and maintaining strong relationships with colleagues, even in a remote work setting. By cultivating a sense of community and support, we can create a positive work environment that promotes growth and collaboration.

Lastly, we will discuss the role of faith in our professional lives. As Christians, we are called to be a light in the workplace, reflecting the love and grace of Christ in our interactions with others. This chapter will provide practical guidance on how to integrate faith into our work, from setting a positive example to sharing our beliefs in a respectful and compassionate manner. By doing so, we can make a lasting impact on our colleagues and contribute to a more inclusive and supportive work environment.

3

Chapter 3: Building Strong Relationships in a Digital Age

The rise of technology has transformed the way we form and maintain relationships. As Christians, we must navigate these changes with wisdom and discernment, ensuring that our relationships are grounded in love, trust, and authenticity. In this chapter, we will explore the impact of technology on our relationships and how we can build strong, meaningful connections in a digital age.

One of the key challenges of digital communication is the potential for miscommunication and misunderstandings. With the absence of non-verbal cues, it can be difficult to accurately convey our thoughts and emotions. This chapter will offer strategies for effective digital communication, emphasizing the importance of clarity, empathy, and active listening. By being intentional in our interactions, we can foster deeper connections and avoid potential conflicts.

In addition to effective communication, we must also be mindful of the influence of social media on our relationships. While social media can be a valuable tool for staying connected with friends and family, it can also contribute to feelings of envy, inadequacy, and isolation. This chapter will discuss the impact of social media on our mental and emotional well-being, and how we can use it in a way that fosters genuine connections and supports our spiritual growth.

Furthermore, we will explore the role of technology in romantic relationships. From online dating to maintaining long-distance relationships, technology has opened up new possibilities for finding and nurturing love. This chapter will provide practical tips for navigating the complexities of digital romance, emphasizing the importance of authenticity, trust, and shared values. By approaching relationships with a Christ-centered mindset, we can build strong, healthy partnerships that honor God and support our personal growth.

Lastly, we will discuss the importance of community and fellowship in a digital age. While technology has made it easier to stay connected, it is essential to prioritize face-to-face interactions and build meaningful relationships within our local communities. This chapter will offer guidance on how to balance online and offline relationships, and the importance of investing in our church and local community. By doing so, we can create a supportive network that encourages spiritual growth and mutual support.

4

Chapter 4: AI and the Future of Work

Artificial intelligence (AI) is transforming the workplace, offering new opportunities and challenges for professionals across various industries. As Christians, we must approach these changes with a sense of curiosity and discernment, seeking to understand the implications of AI on our work and society. In this chapter, we will explore the impact of AI on the future of work, and how we can navigate this evolving landscape with faith and integrity.

One of the key areas where AI is making a significant impact is automation. While automation can increase efficiency and productivity, it also raises concerns about job displacement and the future of work. This chapter will discuss the potential benefits and drawbacks of automation, and how we can prepare for a future where AI plays a central role in our professional lives. By staying informed and adaptable, we can navigate the changing job market and find new opportunities for growth and development.

In addition to automation, AI is also transforming the way we make decisions and solve problems. From data analysis to predictive modeling, AI offers new tools for improving our decision-making processes. This chapter will explore the ethical considerations of using AI in decision-making, and how we can ensure that these technologies are used responsibly and transparently. By adhering to ethical principles and maintaining a human-centered approach, we can harness the power of AI for the greater good.

Furthermore, we must consider the implications of AI on workplace relationships and dynamics. As AI becomes more integrated into our work environments, it is essential to foster a sense of collaboration and trust between humans and machines. This chapter will offer guidance on how to build strong relationships with AI technologies, emphasizing the importance of transparency, accountability, and mutual respect. By working together with AI, we can create a more inclusive and supportive work environment.

Lastly, we will explore the role of faith in navigating the future of work. As Christians, we are called to approach technological advancements with a sense of stewardship and responsibility. This chapter will provide practical tips for integrating faith into our professional lives, from seeking God's guidance in our career decisions to using our skills and talents for the benefit of others. By doing so, we can ensure that our work reflects our values and contributes to a more just and compassionate society.

5

Chapter 5: Ethical Considerations in AI Development

The development and implementation of artificial intelligence (AI) technologies raise a number of ethical considerations that must be carefully examined. As Christians, we have a responsibility to ensure that these technologies are developed and used in a way that aligns with our values and principles. In this chapter, we will explore the ethical considerations of AI development, and how we can advocate for responsible and transparent practices in the field of AI.

One of the key ethical concerns in AI development is the potential for bias and discrimination. AI systems are often trained on large datasets, which can contain biases that are inadvertently incorporated into the algorithms. This chapter will discuss the impact of bias in AI, and how we can work to mitigate these risks through careful design and testing. By promoting diversity and inclusion in AI development, we can create more equitable and fair technologies.

In addition to bias, we must also consider the implications of AI on privacy and data security. As AI systems become more sophisticated, they often require access to large amounts of personal data. This raises concerns about how this data is collected, stored, and used. This chapter will delve into the ethical considerations of data privacy, and how we can ensure that AI technologies are developed and used in a way that respects individuals' rights to privacy. By advocating for strong data protection policies and practices, we can build trust and confidence in AI technologies.

Furthermore, we must consider the potential for AI to be used in ways that harm individuals or society. From surveillance to autonomous weapons, there are a number of applications of AI that raise significant ethical concerns. This chapter will explore the potential risks and harms of AI, and how we can work to prevent the misuse of these technologies. By promoting responsible and transparent AI development, we can ensure that these technologies are developed and used for the benefit of society as a whole. This chapter will provide practical guidance on advocating for ethical AI practices, from participating in public discussions to supporting organizations that promote responsible AI development. By engaging with the broader community, we can help shape the future of AI in a way that reflects our values and principles.

Moreover, we will discuss the importance of transparency and accountability in AI development. As AI technologies become more integrated into our daily lives, it is essential to ensure that they are developed and deployed in a way that is transparent and accountable to the public. This chapter will explore the role of regulation and oversight in promoting ethical AI practices, and how we can advocate for policies that protect individuals and society. By supporting transparency and accountability, we can build trust in AI technologies and ensure that they are used for the greater good.

Lastly, we will consider the role of faith in guiding our approach to AI ethics. As Christians, we are called to act justly and love mercy, and this should inform our approach to AI development. This chapter will provide practical tips for integrating faith into our work in AI, from seeking God's guidance in our decisions to using our skills and talents to promote ethical practices. By grounding our work in faith, we can ensure that our contributions to AI development reflect our values and principles.

6

Chapter 6: AI in Ministry and Outreach

Artificial intelligence (AI) has the potential to revolutionize ministry and outreach, offering new tools and opportunities for sharing the Gospel and serving others. In this chapter, we will explore the ways in which AI can be used to enhance ministry and outreach efforts, and how we can harness its potential for the Kingdom of God.

One of the key areas where AI can be used in ministry is in data analysis and decision-making. From analyzing demographic data to predicting trends, AI can provide valuable insights that inform our ministry strategies and outreach efforts. This chapter will discuss practical applications of AI in ministry, and how we can use these tools to better understand and serve our communities. By leveraging AI, we can make more informed decisions that maximize our impact and reach.

In addition to data analysis, AI can also be used to enhance communication and engagement in ministry. From chatbots that provide instant support to automated communication tools, AI can help us connect with people more effectively and efficiently. This chapter will explore the potential of AI-powered communication tools in ministry, and how we can use them to build stronger relationships and foster a sense of community. By embracing AI, we can create more meaningful and engaging ministry experiences.

Furthermore, we must consider the ethical implications of using AI in ministry and outreach. As with any technology, it is essential to use AI responsibly and ethically, ensuring that it is used in a way that respects individuals' rights and dignity. This chapter will discuss the ethical considerations of using AI in ministry, from data privacy to the potential for bias. By approaching AI with a Christ-centered mindset, we can ensure that our ministry efforts reflect our values and principles.

Lastly, we will explore the role of faith in guiding our use of AI in ministry. As Christians, we are called to share the love of Christ and serve others, and AI can be a powerful tool for fulfilling this mission. This chapter will provide practical tips for integrating AI into our ministry efforts, from seeking God's guidance in our decisions to using AI to support our spiritual growth. By grounding our use of AI in faith, we can ensure that our ministry efforts are effective and aligned with our calling.

7

Chapter 7: Balancing Technology and Spiritual Growth

In a world where technology is ever-present, it is essential to find a balance that supports our spiritual growth and well-being. As Christians, we must navigate the digital landscape with discernment, ensuring that our use of technology enhances our relationship with God and others. In this chapter, we will explore practical strategies for balancing technology and spiritual growth.

One of the key challenges of our digital age is the potential for technology to distract us from our spiritual practices. From constant notifications to endless entertainment options, it can be difficult to find time for prayer, reflection, and worship. This chapter will offer practical tips for managing digital distractions, from setting boundaries to creating technology-free spaces. By being intentional in our use of technology, we can create a more focused and meaningful spiritual life.

In addition to managing distractions, we must also consider the potential for technology to enhance our spiritual practices. From digital devotionals to online prayer groups, technology can provide new opportunities for connecting with God and others. This chapter will explore the potential of digital tools for spiritual growth, and how we can use them to support our faith journey. By leveraging technology in a way that aligns with our values, we can create a more vibrant and connected spiritual life.

Furthermore, we must consider the impact of technology on our mental and emotional well-being. While technology can provide valuable resources and support, it can also contribute to feelings of anxiety, isolation, and stress. This chapter will discuss the importance of self-care and mental health in a digital age, and how we can create a healthy balance that supports our overall well-being. By prioritizing self-care and seeking support when needed, we can ensure that our use of technology is beneficial and sustainable.

Lastly, we will explore the role of community in balancing technology and spiritual growth. As Christians, we are called to live in community and support one another in our faith journeys. This chapter will provide practical tips for building and maintaining strong relationships within our church and local communities, and how we can support one another in navigating the digital landscape. By fostering a sense of community and mutual support, we can create a more balanced and fulfilling spiritual life.

8

Chapter 8: Raising Children in a Digital World

Raising children in a digital world presents unique challenges and opportunities for Christian parents. As technology continues to shape our lives, it is essential to guide our children in navigating this landscape with wisdom and discernment. In this chapter, we will explore practical strategies for raising children in a digital world, and how we can instill values and principles that support their spiritual growth.

One of the key challenges of raising children in a digital age is managing screen time and ensuring that technology is used in a balanced and healthy way. This chapter will offer practical tips for setting boundaries and creating technology-free zones in the home. By establishing clear guidelines and promoting healthy habits, we can help our children develop a balanced relationship with technology.

In addition to managing screen time, we must also consider the impact of technology on our children's mental and emotional well-being. From social media to online gaming, technology can expose children to a range of influences and experiences. This chapter will discuss the potential risks and benefits of digital media, and how we can support our children in navigating these challenges. By fostering open communication and providing guidance, we can help our children build resilience and make informed choices.

Furthermore, we must consider the role of technology in our children's spiritual development. From online devotionals to virtual Sunday school classes, technology can provide valuable resources for nurturing their faith. This chapter will explore the potential of digital tools for supporting our children's spiritual growth, and how we can integrate these resources into our family life. By creating a Christ-centered digital environment, we can help our children develop a strong foundation of faith.

Lastly, we will discuss the importance of modeling healthy technology use for our children. As parents, we play a crucial role in shaping our children's attitudes and behaviors towards technology. This chapter will provide practical tips for setting a positive example and creating a family culture that values balance, integrity, and spiritual growth. By modeling healthy technology use and prioritizing our faith, we can guide our children in navigating the digital world with wisdom and discernment.

9

Chapter 9: The Role of AI in Healthcare

Artificial intelligence (AI) has the potential to revolutionize healthcare, offering new tools and opportunities for improving patient care and outcomes. As Christians, we must navigate these advancements with discernment, ensuring that they align with our values and principles. In this chapter, we will explore the impact of AI on healthcare, and how we can approach these changes with faith and integrity.

One of the key areas where AI is making a significant impact is in diagnostics and treatment. From imaging analysis to predictive modeling, AI can provide valuable insights that improve the accuracy and efficiency of medical care. This chapter will discuss practical applications of AI in healthcare, and how we can ensure that these technologies are used responsibly and ethically. By promoting transparency and accountability, we can build trust in AI-powered healthcare solutions.

In addition to diagnostics and treatment, AI is also transforming the way we manage patient data and records. From electronic health records to data analysis, AI can streamline administrative processes and improve the quality of care. This chapter will explore the potential benefits and drawbacks of AI in healthcare administration, and how we can ensure that patient privacy and data security are prioritized. By advocating for strong data protection policies, we can ensure that AI technologies are used in a way that respects individuals' rights and dignity.

Furthermore, we must consider the ethical implications of using AI in healthcare, particularly in relation to patient consent and autonomy. As AI becomes more integrated into medical decision-making, it is essential to ensure that patients are fully informed and involved in their care. This chapter will discuss the importance of patient-centered care, and how we can ensure that AI technologies support, rather than undermine, patient autonomy. By fostering open communication and collaboration, we can create a healthcare system that prioritizes patient well-being and dignity.

Lastly, we will explore the role of faith in navigating the impact of AI on healthcare. As Christians, we are called to care for the sick and vulnerable, and AI can be a powerful tool for fulfilling this mission. This chapter will provide practical tips for integrating faith into our approach to AI in healthcare, from seeking God's guidance in our decisions to using AI to support compassionate and patient-centered care. By grounding our use of AI in faith, we can ensure that our contributions to healthcare reflect our values and principles.

10

Chapter 10: AI and Education

Artificial intelligence (AI) is transforming the field of education, offering new tools and opportunities for enhancing learning and teaching. As Christians, we must approach these advancements with a sense of curiosity and discernment, ensuring that they align with our values and principles. In this chapter, we will explore the impact of AI on education, and how we can harness its potential for the benefit of students and educators.

One of the key areas where AI is making a significant impact is in personalized learning. From adaptive learning platforms to AI-powered tutoring, technology can provide tailored educational experiences that meet the unique needs of each student. This chapter will discuss practical applications of AI in personalized learning, and how we can ensure that these technologies are used responsibly and ethically. By promoting equity and inclusion, we can create more accessible and effective educational experiences.

In addition to personalized learning, AI is also transforming the way we assess and evaluate student performance. From automated grading to predictive analytics, AI can provide valuable insights that inform instructional strategies and support student growth. This chapter will explore the potential benefits and drawbacks of AI in assessment, and how we can ensure that these technologies are used in a way that respects student privacy and dignity.

By advocating for transparency and accountability, we can build trust in AI-powered educational solutions.

Furthermore, we must consider the ethical implications of using AI in education, particularly in relation to data privacy and security. As AI systems become more integrated into educational environments, it is essential to ensure that student data is collected, stored, and used in a way that respects individuals' rights and dignity. This chapter will discuss the importance of strong data protection policies, and how we can ensure that AI technologies are used responsibly and ethically in education.

Lastly, we will explore the role of faith in guiding our approach to AI in education. As Christians, we are called to seek wisdom and understanding, and AI can be a powerful tool for supporting this mission. This chapter will provide practical tips for integrating faith into our approach to AI in education, from seeking God's guidance in our decisions to using AI to support inclusive and effective educational experiences. By grounding our use of AI in faith, we can ensure that our contributions to education reflect our values and principles.

11

Chapter 11: The Future of AI and the Church

As artificial intelligence (AI) continues to evolve, it presents new opportunities and challenges for the Church. As Christians, we must approach these advancements with discernment and faith, ensuring that they align with our mission and values. In this chapter, we will explore the impact of AI on the Church, and how we can harness its potential for ministry and outreach.

One of the key areas where AI can be used in the Church is in enhancing communication and engagement. From AI-powered chatbots to automated communication tools, technology can help us connect with people more effectively and efficiently. This chapter will explore the potential of AI-powered communication tools in ministry, and how we can use them to build stronger relationships and foster a sense of community. By embracing AI, we can create more meaningful and engaging ministry experiences.

In addition to communication, AI can also be used to support ministry and outreach efforts through data analysis and decision-making. From analyzing demographic data to predicting trends, AI can provide valuable insights that inform our ministry strategies and outreach efforts. This chapter will discuss practical applications of AI in ministry, and how we can use these tools to better understand and serve our communities. By leveraging AI, we can make more informed decisions that maximize our impact and reach.

Furthermore, we must consider the ethical implications of using AI in the Church, particularly in relation to data privacy and security. As AI systems become more integrated into ministry environments, it is essential to ensure that data is collected, stored, and used in a way that respects individuals' rights and dignity. This chapter will discuss the importance of strong data protection policies, and how we can ensure that AI technologies are used responsibly and ethically in the Church.

Lastly, we will explore the role of faith in guiding our use of AI in the Church. As Christians, we are called to share the love of Christ and serve others, and AI can be a powerful tool for fulfilling this mission. This chapter will provide practical tips for integrating AI into our ministry efforts, from seeking God's guidance in our decisions to using AI to support our spiritual growth. By grounding our use of AI in faith, we can ensure that our ministry efforts are effective and aligned with our calling.

12

Chapter 12: Embracing the Future with Faith

As we look to the future, it is clear that artificial intelligence (AI) will continue to play a significant role in shaping our world. As Christians, we must approach these changes with a sense of faith and discernment, ensuring that our use of AI aligns with our values and principles. In this final chapter, we will explore how we can embrace the future with faith, leveraging AI for the greater good.

One of the key challenges of embracing the future with AI is navigating the ethical and moral implications of these technologies. From issues of privacy and security to questions of bias and fairness, it is essential to approach AI with a sense of responsibility and stewardship. This chapter will provide practical guidance on how to navigate these ethical considerations, from advocating for responsible AI development to promoting transparency and accountability. By doing so, we can ensure that AI technologies are used in a way that benefits society as a whole.

In addition to ethical considerations, we must also consider the impact of AI on our personal and spiritual lives. From managing digital distractions to fostering meaningful connections, it is essential to find a balance that supports our well-being and spiritual growth. This chapter will offer practical tips for integrating AI into our daily lives in a way that enhances our relationship with God and others. By approaching AI with a Christ-centered mindset, we can ensure that our use of technology supports our faith journey.

Furthermore, we must consider the role of community and collaboration in embracing the future with AI. As Christians, we are called to live in community and support one another in our faith journeys. This chapter will explore the importance of building strong relationships within our church and local communities, and how we can support one another in navigating the digital landscape. By fostering a sense of community and mutual support, we can create a more balanced and fulfilling spiritual life.

Lastly, we will explore the importance of seeking God's guidance as we navigate the future with AI. As Christians, we are called to seek wisdom and understanding, and AI can be a powerful tool for supporting this mission. This chapter will provide practical tips for seeking God's guidance in our use of AI, from prayer and reflection to seeking counsel from trusted mentors. By grounding our use of AI in faith, we can ensure that our contributions to the future reflect our values and principles.

13

Chapter 13: AI and the Environment

Artificial intelligence (AI) has the potential to play a significant role in addressing environmental challenges and promoting sustainability. As Christians, we have a responsibility to care for God's creation and ensure that our use of technology aligns with this calling. In this chapter, we will explore the impact of AI on the environment, and how we can leverage its potential for the benefit of our planet.

One of the key areas where AI can be used to support environmental sustainability is in resource management. From optimizing energy usage to monitoring natural resources, AI can provide valuable insights that help us make more informed decisions. This chapter will discuss practical applications of AI in resource management, and how we can ensure that these technologies are used responsibly and ethically. By promoting sustainable practices, we can reduce our environmental footprint and protect the planet for future generations.

In addition to resource management, AI can also be used to address environmental challenges such as climate change and pollution. From predictive modeling to data analysis, AI can help us better understand and mitigate the impact of these issues. This chapter will explore the potential of AI in addressing environmental challenges, and how we can ensure that these technologies are used in a way that supports our commitment to environmental stewardship. By leveraging AI, we can make a positive impact on the environment and promote a more sustainable future.

Furthermore, we must consider the ethical implications of using AI in environmental initiatives, particularly in relation to data privacy and security. As AI systems become more integrated into environmental monitoring and management, it is essential to ensure that data is collected, stored, and used in a way that respects individuals' rights and dignity. This chapter will discuss the importance of strong data protection policies, and how we can ensure that AI technologies are used responsibly and ethically in environmental initiatives.

Lastly, we will explore the role of faith in guiding our approach to AI and the environment. As Christians, we are called to be stewards of God's creation, and AI can be a powerful tool for fulfilling this mission. This chapter will provide practical tips for integrating faith into our approach to AI and environmental sustainability, from seeking God's guidance in our decisions to using AI to support our commitment to environmental stewardship. By grounding our use of AI in faith, we can ensure that our contributions to environmental initiatives reflect our values and principles.

14

Chapter 14: AI and Humanitarian Aid

Artificial intelligence (AI) has the potential to revolutionize humanitarian aid efforts, offering new tools and opportunities for supporting vulnerable populations and addressing global challenges. As Christians, we are called to care for those in need, and AI can be a powerful tool for fulfilling this mission. In this chapter, we will explore the impact of AI on humanitarian aid, and how we can leverage its potential for the benefit of others.

One of the key areas where AI can be used in humanitarian aid is in disaster response and recovery. From predictive modeling to real-time data analysis, AI can provide valuable insights that improve the efficiency and effectiveness of humanitarian efforts. This chapter will discuss practical applications of AI in disaster response, and how we can ensure that these technologies are used responsibly and ethically. By leveraging AI, we can save lives and support communities in times of crisis.

In addition to disaster response, AI can also be used to address long-term humanitarian challenges such as poverty, hunger, and access to healthcare. From data analysis to resource allocation, AI can help us better understand and address the root causes of these issues. This chapter will explore the potential of AI in addressing humanitarian challenges, and how we can ensure that these technologies are used in a way that supports our commitment to justice and compassion. By leveraging AI, we can make a positive impact on vulnerable populations and promote a more just and equitable world.

Furthermore, we must consider the ethical implications of using AI in humanitarian aid, particularly in relation to data privacy and security. As AI systems become more integrated into humanitarian initiatives, it is essential to ensure that data is collected, stored, and used in a way that respects individuals' rights and dignity. This chapter will discuss the importance of strong data protection policies, and how we can ensure that AI technologies are used responsibly and ethically in humanitarian aid.

Lastly, we will explore the role of faith in guiding our approach to AI and humanitarian aid. As Christians, we are called to love our neighbors and care for those in need, and AI can be a powerful tool for fulfilling this mission. This chapter will provide practical tips for integrating faith into our approach to AI and humanitarian aid, from seeking God's guidance in our decisions to using AI to support our commitment to justice and compassion. By grounding our use of AI in faith, we can ensure that our contributions to humanitarian initiatives reflect our values and principles.

15

Chapter 15: AI and Mental Health

Artificial intelligence (AI) has the potential to revolutionize mental health care, offering new tools and opportunities for supporting individuals and addressing mental health challenges. As Christians, we have a responsibility to care for our own mental health and support others in their mental health journeys. In this chapter, we will explore the impact of AI on mental health, and how we can leverage its potential for the benefit of individuals and communities.

One of the key areas where AI can be used in mental health care is in early detection and intervention. From predictive modeling to digital assessments, AI can provide valuable insights that improve the accuracy and timeliness of mental health care. This chapter will discuss practical applications of AI in early detection and intervention, and how we can ensure that these technologies are used responsibly and ethically. By leveraging AI, we can provide more effective and compassionate mental health care.

In addition to early detection, AI can also be used to support ongoing mental health care and treatment. From AI-powered therapy to digital support tools, technology can provide valuable resources that enhance the quality and accessibility of mental health care. This chapter will explore the potential of AI in supporting mental health care, and how we can ensure that these technologies are used in a way that respects individuals' rights and dignity. By advocating for responsible and ethical AI practices, we can create a more supportive and inclusive mental health care system.

Furthermore, we must consider the ethical implications of using AI in mental health care, particularly in relation to data privacy and security. As AI systems become more integrated into mental health care environments, it is essential to ensure that data is collected, stored, and used in a way that respects individuals' rights and dignity. This chapter will discuss the importance of strong data protection policies, and how we can ensure that AI technologies are used responsibly and ethically in mental health care.

Lastly, we will explore the role of faith in guiding our approach to AI and mental health. As Christians, we are called to care for our own mental health and support others in their mental health journeys, and AI can be a powerful tool for fulfilling this mission. This chapter will provide practical tips for integrating faith into our approach to AI and mental health, from seeking God's guidance in our decisions to using AI to support our mental health care. By grounding our use of AI in faith, we can ensure that our contributions to mental health care reflect our values and principles.

16

Chapter 16: AI and Ethical Leadership

In a world where artificial intelligence (AI) is becoming increasingly integrated into our lives, ethical leadership is more important than ever. As Christians, we have a responsibility to lead with integrity and ensure that our use of AI aligns with our values and principles. In this final chapter, we will explore the importance of ethical leadership in the age of AI, and how we can cultivate these qualities in ourselves and others.

One of the key aspects of ethical leadership is the ability to navigate complex ethical dilemmas and make informed decisions that reflect our values. This chapter will discuss the importance of ethical decision-making in the context of AI, and how we can develop the skills and knowledge needed to lead with integrity. By promoting transparency and accountability, we can build trust and credibility in our use of AI.

In addition to ethical decision-making, we must also consider the role of empathy and compassion in ethical leadership. As leaders, we are called to care for others and ensure that our use of AI supports their well-being and dignity. This chapter will explore the importance of empathy and compassion in ethical leadership, and how we can cultivate these qualities in our interactions with others. By fostering a sense of care and concern, we can create a more inclusive and supportive environment.

Furthermore, we must consider the importance of community and collaboration in ethical leadership. As Christians, we are called to live in community and support one another in our faith journeys. This chapter will discuss the importance of building strong relationships within our teams and organizations, and how we can support one another in navigating the ethical challenges of AI. By fostering a sense of community and mutual support, we can create a more balanced and fulfilling work environment.

Lastly, we will explore the role of faith in guiding our approach to ethical leadership. As Christians, we are called to seek wisdom and understanding, and AI can be a powerful tool for supporting this mission. This chapter will provide practical tips for integrating faith into our approach to ethical leadership, from seeking God's guidance in our decisions to using AI to support our commitment to integrity and justice. By grounding our leadership in faith, we can ensure that our contributions to the future reflect our values and principles.

In a world increasingly dominated by technology, how do Christians navigate the digital landscape while staying true to their faith? "**From Silicon to Soul: A Christian's Guide to Career, Relationships, and AI**" explores the intersection of technology, faith, and everyday life, providing practical advice and insights for Christians seeking to thrive in the modern world.

This comprehensive guide covers a range of topics, from ethical considerations in AI development to the impact of technology on relationships, mental health, and the environment. Each chapter delves into the challenges and opportunities presented by digital advancements, offering faith-based perspectives and actionable strategies for integrating technology into our personal and professional lives.

Whether you're navigating the digital workplace, building strong relationships in an online world, or leveraging AI for ministry and outreach, this book provides the tools and guidance you need to make informed decisions that align with your values and principles. With a focus on balancing technology and spiritual growth, "From Silicon to Soul" empowers Christians to embrace the future with faith and integrity, ensuring that their use of technology reflects their commitment to justice, compassion, and stewardship.

www.ingramcontent.com/pod-product-compliance
Lightning Source LLC
LaVergne TN
LVHW020500080526
838202LV00057B/6074